101 REASONS

· TO HAVE A ·

PINT OF
BEER

AND A BARREL LOAD OF

Nonsense

Published in 2016 by Baker & Taylor UK Ltd
Bicester, Oxfordshire OX26 4ST

Manuscript by Roffy
Contents layout: seagulls.net
Cover design: Milestone Creative

ISBN 978-1-910562-35-2

Printed in China

101 REASONS

· TO HAVE A ·

PINT OF
BEER

AND A BARREL LOAD OF

Nonsense

This book is dedicated to my mum, Barbara, who will be not be surprised to read that I enjoy beer.

(With thanks to my local, The Horse and Jockey in Penn, for providing several pints of inspiration.)

ANYONE FANCY A PINT?

Friday has arrived. It's been a hard week. It's time for a beer.

But whether you are in the mood for a bottle at home or a pint down the pub, there's that little nagging voice again. Be it your conscience or your better half, the voice is asking, 'Why do you want a beer?'

Well now the answer to that question is at hand. In fact, 101 answers.

Whatever your situation, one of these carefully crafted, scientifically proven reasons to have a pint of beer will prove the perfect retort.

Not only that, but you are holding three books in one. Because alongside the reasons are 101 hand-pulled beer facts.

In these pages you will discover:

— Where you can find beer on the moon

— Which parts of a fish help make beer

— Why you might enjoy the company of a 'small humble wolf'

And last and by no means least, we present some export-strength one-liners, jokes, proverbs and quotes from beer lovers throughout the ages. Right from the earliest philosophers to today's celebs - all offering their wit and wisdom in honour of the hop.

So grab yourself a pint glass, fill it with your favourite brew, sit back and enjoy *101 Reasons To Have A Pint of Beer*.

CHEERS!

REASON #1

BECAUSE THE PUB WILL
CLOSE
IN FIVE HOURS.

BEER FACT

When Niels Bohr won a Nobel Prize in 1922, Carlsberg gave him a house next to the brewery with free beer on tap.

DOCTOR: The best thing for you is to give up beer,
get up early each morning and go to bed early each night.

PATIENT: What's the second best thing?

REASON #2

IN TERMS OF

CHEMISTRY,

BEER IS A

SOLUTION.

BEER FACT

THE WORLD'S STRONGEST BEER, BREWMEISTER'S 'SNAKE VENOM', HAS AN ABV OF 67.5%.

Morse poured himself a can of beer. 'Champagne's a lovely drink, but it makes you thirsty, doesn't it?'

COLIN DEXTER, *THE WAY THROUGH THE WOODS*

REASON #3
AFTER THE GARDENING I NEED TO PLANT MYSELF ON THE
SOFA.

BEER FACT
VIKINGS DRANK BEER FROM THE SKULLS OF THEIR ENEMIES.

Fermentation and civilization are inseparable.

JOHN CIARDI

Beer is a wholesome liquor ... it abounds with nourishment.

DR BENJAMIN RUSH

REASON #4

OTHERWISE IT'S NOT A PROPER BARBECUE.

BEER FACT

MARINATING BEEF STEAK IN BEER CAN COUNTER 70 PER CENT OF THE CARCINOGENS.

Shoulder the sky, my lad, and drink your ale.

A. E. HOUSMAN

It takes beer to make thirst worthwhile.

GERMAN PROVERB

REASON #5

BECAUSE ABSTINENCE IS BEST PRACTISED IN MODERATION.

BEER FACT

THE ABASHIRI BREWERY IN JAPAN MAKES ITS OKHOTSK BLUE DRAFT BEER FROM ICEBERGS.

Wherever beer is brewed, all is well. Wherever beer is drunk, life is good.

CZECH PROVERB

Beer makes you feel the way you ought to feel without beer.

HENRY LAWSON

REASON #6

I'M GIVING IN TO
BEER
PRESSURE.

BEER FACT

Salt in water used for brewing beer will intensify the flavour. However, too much will kill the yeast.

A little bit of beer is divine medicine.

PARACELSUS, GREEK PHYSICIAN

Beer drinkin' don't do half the harm of love makin'.

ALEXANDER POPE

REASON #7

HAPPY BIRTHDAY

TO 1/365TH OF THE PLANET!

BEER FACT

A 'TYG' IS A LARGE ENGLISH POTTERY MUG WITH UP TO SIX HANDLES DESIGNED FOR TRULY CONVIVIAL OCCASIONS.

In my opinion, most of the great men of the past were only there for the beer – the wealth, prestige and grandeur that went with the power.

A. J. P. TAYLOR

REASON #8
THE BARMAID ENJOYS MY
WITTY REPARTEE.

BEER FACT
BEER SERVED BELOW 4 DEGREES CENTIGRADE WILL HAVE NEXT TO NO TASTE.

Englishmen are like their own beer: frothy on top, dregs on the bottom, the middle excellent.

VOLTAIRE

You can't drink all day if you don't start in the morning.

FROM THE LABEL ON A BOTTLE OF *BREAKFAST STOUT*

REASON #9

I FANCY A BLONDE.

BEER FACT

Whiskey maker Jim Beam attempted to block imports of Irish stout Beamish, fearing it would confuse US consumers.

Cover a war in a place where you can't drink beer or talk to a woman? Hell no!

HUNTER S. THOMPSON

There is no such thing as a bad beer. It's that some taste better than others.

BILLY CARTER

REASON #10

IF I DON'T DRINK IT, IT WILL

GO OFF.

BEER FACT

BROWN GLASS IS BEST FOR BEER BOTTLES AS IT FILTERS OUT LIGHT WHICH WOULD OTHERWISE BREAK DOWN HOPS.

Let a man walk ten miles steadily on a hot summer's day along a dusty English road, and he will soon discover why beer was invented.

G. K. CHESTERTON

Indeed, beer has been the only thing that has permitted generations of Englishmen to endure the cooking of English cooks without murdering them.

ANON

REASON #11

THAT BARREL LOOKS A
BIT FULL.

BEER FACT

FIRKIN COMES FROM THE OLD DUTCH WORD 'VIERDEKIJN' MEANING 'FOURTH' AS A FIRKIN IS ONE-FOURTH OF A BARREL.

On the chest of a barmaid in Sale
were tattooed all the prices of ale.
And on her behind,
for the sake of the blind,
was the same information in Braille.

REASON #12

WHAT ELSE CAN I DO BEFORE THE CURRY ARRIVES?

BEER FACT

Joseph Priestly noticed that the gas given off from fermenting beer drifted to the ground, helping him discover carbon dioxide.

I work until beer o'clock.
STEPHEN KING

I have respect for beer.
RUSSELL CROWE

REASON #13

THE GLASS STICKS TO THE TABLE UNLESS I KEEP LIFTING IT.

BEER FACT

Yeast likes copper. Stainless steel breweries often install lengths of copper pipe to help with the brew.

BEER: THE METHOD OF TURNING GRAIN INTO URINE.

REASON #14

THE TV IN THIS ROOM ONLY HAS FOUR CHANNELS – AND THEY'RE ALL GERMAN.

BEER FACT

BAVARIAN BEER WEEK OPENS WITH A FOUNTAIN DISPENSING FREE BEER TO THE PUBLIC.

Ale is meat, drink and cloth; it will make a cat speak and a wise man dumb.

JONATHAN SWIFT

I don't think I've drunk enough beer to understand that.

TERRY PRATCHETT

REASON #15

MY MOTHER-IN-LAW IS SAFELY ON A TRAIN HOME.

BEER FACT

For a month after a Babylonian wedding, the bride's father would supply his son-in-law with all the mead, or honey beer, he could drink. This was known as the 'honey month', now the 'honeymoon'.

WHOEVER MAKES A POOR BEER IS TRANSFERRED TO THE DUNG-HILL.

EDICT FROM THE CITY OF DANZIG, 11TH CENTURY

REASON #16

THE NEWSPAPER SAID IT WAS A SUPERFOOD.

BEER FACT

BELGIANS EAT HOPS WITH A WARM SAUCE OF BUTTER AND CRÈME FRAÎCHE.

Water is good for only two things: floating ships and making beer.

KEN JONES

If God had intended us to drink beer, He would have given us stomachs.

DAVID DAYE

REASON #17

IT'S MY FAVOURITE SAINT'S DAY.

BEER FACT

IN 1759 ARTHUR GUINNESS SIGNED A 9,000-YEAR LEASE FOR ST JAMES'S GATE BREWERY, AT £45 PER ANNUM.

Ale sellers should not be taletellers.

SCOTTISH PROVERB

Beer, it's the best damn drink in the world.

JACK NICHOLSON

REASON #18

YOU MIGHT CALL IT

BEER,

BUT I CALL IT

DINNER.

BEER FACT

GRAINS WERE BEING USED IN BEER 2,000 YEARS BEFORE THEY WERE USED IN BREAD.

You can never be sure how many beers you had last night.

THE HEINEKEN UNCERTAINTY PRINCIPLE

REASON #19
MY ELBOW NEEDS THE
EXERCISE.

BEER FACT
THERE IS NO CORRELATION BETWEEN DRINKING BEER AND HAVING A BEER BELLY.

I dropped into The Plough at Cadsden for a pint of IPA and some fish and chips with China's President Xi.

AS TWEETED BY DAVID CAMERON

My favourite food from my homeland is Guinness. My second choice in Guinness. My third choice – would have to be Guinness.

PETER O'TOOLE

REASON #20

I'M TRYING TO STOP YEAST FROM TAKING OVER THE WORLD.

BEER FACT

A SOUR OR INAPPROPRIATELY BITTER TASTE IN BEER IS KNOWN AS 'YEAST BITE'.

Water? But water is not fit for men to drink. For the cattle, for birds and beast, but a man needs ale ... or wine, if you are a Frenchman.

LOUIS L'AMOUR, *TO THE FAR BLUE MOUNTAINS*

REASON #21

THE LANDLORD HAS KIDS TO GET THROUGH UNIVERSITY.

BEER FACT

IN THE 1800s, STRONG ALE WAS KNOWN AS 'NAPPY' BECAUSE TWO PINTS WOULD MAKE YOU SLEEPY.

He that drinks strong beer,
and goes to bed mellow,
lives as he ought to live,
and dies a hearty fellow.

17TH-CENTURY ENGLISH DRINKING SONG

REASON #22

I NEED A 'HOPPY' ENDING.

BEER FACT

The oldest known beer advertisement was found on a clay tablet dating from around 4000 BC. It read: 'Drink Ebla – the beer with the heart of a lion'.

Real ale fans are just like train-spotters, only drunk.

CHRISTOPHER HOWSE

Give me a woman who loves beer and I will conquer the world.

KAISER WILHELM

REASON #23

I'M PARTIAL TO A
PORTER.

BEER FACT

PORTER WAS ORIGINALLY A COMBINATION OF THREE BEERS, MIXED AT THE TIME OF SERVICE.

You can only drink 30 or 40 glasses of beer a day, no matter how rich you are.

ADOLPHUS BUSCH

Across the troubled maelstrom of time, people always need a beer.

ELLEN KUSHNER

REASON #24

I'M CURRENTLY IN THE PLANNING STAGES OF A HANGOVER.

BEER FACT

PORTER GETS ITS NAME FROM THE LONDON MARKET PORTERS WHO ENJOYED A PINT DURING THEIR LUNCH BREAK.

I sometimes think the Labour Party is like a pub where the mild is running out. If someone doesn't do something soon, all that's left will be bitter. And all that's bitter will be Left.

MARGARET THATCHER

REASON #25

IT'S
BEER
AWARENESS WEEK.

BEER FACT

634 MILLION PINTS OF CASK ALE ARE CONSUMED IN THE UK EVERY YEAR.

It is my design to die in the brew-house;
let ale be placed to my mouth when I am expiring,
that when the choirs of angels come,
they may say, 'Be God propitious to this drinker.'

SAINT COLUMBANUS, AD 612

REASON #26

MY LUGGAGE IS ON THE WAY TO MINSK.

BEER FACT

THERE IS A CRATER ON THE MOON CALLED BEER.

When the bee comes to your house, let her have beer; you may want to visit the bee's house some day.

CONGOLESE PROVERB

My goal is to hit the gym every day I'm on vacation. Usually I just end up sleeping and drinking beer.

GARY ALLAN

REASON #27

I'M CELEBRATING A TEXTBOOK HILL START.

BEER FACT

Following the D-Day landings, beer was exported to troops in Normandy inside the auxiliary fuel tanks of Spitfires. They were labelled 'Modification XXX Depth Charge' in order to get official approval.

KIRK: Romulan Ale ... Why Bones, you know this is illegal.

BONES: I only use it for medicinal purposes.

FROM THE FILM *STAR TREK: THE WRATH OF KHAN*

REASON #28

IT HELPS ME SEE DOUBLE AND FEEL SINGLE.

BEER FACT

1,000 YEARS AGO, NEARLY ALL OF THE BEER IN EUROPE WAS BREWED WITHOUT HOPS.

Mike Hammer drinks beer because I can't spell Cognac.

MICKEY SPILLANE

Milk is for babies. When you grow up you have to drink beer.

ARNOLD SCHWARZENEGGER

REASON #29

I GAVE UP
EVERYTHING ELSE FOR
LENT.

BEER FACT

Wassail is a spiced honey ale drunk during Yuletide celebrations. The name comes from the Old Norse 'ves heil' meaning 'you be healthy'.

MY BEER IS NOT HALF EMPTY. I'M HALFWAY TO ANOTHER BEER.

REASON #30

I'M ONE-SIXTEENTH BELGIAN.

BEER FACT

THE LATTICEWORK OF FOAM LEFT ON A GLASS AFTER DRINKING BEER IS KNOWN AS BELGIAN (OR BRUSSELS) LACE.

I am a firm believer in the people. If given the truth, they can be depended upon to meet any national crisis. The great point is to bring them the real facts, and beer.

ABRAHAM LINCOLN

REASON #31

OTHERWISE WHAT'S THE POINT OF HOPS?

BEER FACT

HOPS ARE A BETTER SOURCE OF POTENT ANTIOXIDANTS THAN RED WINE, GREEN TEA OR SOY PRODUCTS.

The government will fall that raises the price of beer.

CZECH SAYING

Anyone can drink beer, but it takes intelligence to enjoy beer.

STEPHEN BEAUMONT

REASON #32

I'VE JUST REALISED THIS
GOATEE
IS A BAD IDEA.

BEER FACT

162,719 PINTS OF GUINNESS ARE LOST TO FACIAL HAIR EACH YEAR IN THE UK.

You can't be a real country unless you have a beer and an airline – it helps if you have some kind of a football team, or some nuclear weapons, but at the very least you need a beer.

FRANK ZAPPA

REASON #33

MY PERSONAL FUEL INDICATOR IS LOW.

BEER FACT

THERE ARE TYPICALLY BETWEEN 130 AND 250 CALORIES IN A PINT OF BEER, DEPENDING ON THE STYLE AND STRENGTH.

Six pints of bitter, and quickly please, the world's about to end.

DOUGLAS ADAMS, *HITCHHIKER'S GUIDE TO THE GALAXY*

REASON #34

IT'S WHAT
HALF-TIME
WAS INVENTED FOR.

BEER FACT

THE VELTINS-ARENA, HOME OF THE SCHALKE 04 FOOTBALL CLUB IN GERMANY, HAS A 5KM-LONG BEER PIPELINE.

What event is more awfully important to an English colony than the erection of its first brewhouse?

REVEREND SYDNEY SMITH

Give my people plenty of beer, good beer, and cheap beer, and you will have no revolution among them.

QUEEN VICTORIA

REASON #35

THE POSTER
MADE IT LOOK LIKE A
GREAT IDEA.

BEER FACT

UK ADVERTS CANNOT SHOW ALCOHOL CONSUMPTION AS LEADING TO SOCIAL OR SEXUAL SUCCESS.

Some people wanted Champagne and caviar when they should have had beer and hot dogs.

DWIGHT D. EISENHOWER

Beer may not help me do things better, but it makes me less ashamed of doing them badly.

ANON

REASON #36

THE WAY TO MY HEART IS VIA MY LIVER.

BEER FACT

THE FIRST PROFESSIONAL BREWERS, KNOWN AS 'SABTIEM', WERE ALL WOMEN.

LADY NANCY ASTOR: I would rather commit adultery than drink a glass of beer.

A VOICE FROM THE CROWD: Who wouldn't?

REASON #37

IT'S ON MY 'TO DO' LIST.

BEER FACT

Before reliable thermometers, brewers used to ensure their brew was not too hot by dipping in their thumb, leading to the phrase 'The Rule of Thumb'.

IF YOU GUYS ARE GOING TO BE THROWING BEER BOTTLES AT US, AT LEAST MAKE SURE THEY'RE FULL.

DAVE MUSTAINE, OF THE BAND MEGADETH

REASON #38

WHO CAN RESIST A BEER CALLED 'HOPTIMUS PRIME'?

BEER FACT

The 'Description of Britaine' from 1596 lists beers such as 'Go By The Wall', 'Dragon's Milke' and 'Father Whoresonne'.

Why is Australian beer served cold? So you can tell it from urine.

DAVID MOULTON

Ere's to English women an' a quart of English beer.

RUDYARD KIPLING

REASON #39

PLANTING
MORE HOPS IS GOOD FOR THE
ENVIRONMENT.

BEER FACT

Bohemian hops were so prized that King Wenceslas ordered the death penalty for anyone caught exporting hops or cuttings.

The first draught serveth for health, the second for pleasure, the third for shame, the fourth for madness.

SIR WALTER RALEIGH

I'm an old-fashioned guy ... I want to be an old man with a beer belly sitting on a porch, looking at a lake or something.

JOHNNY DEPP

REASON #40

I NEED TO GET STRAIGHT TO THE PINT.

BEER FACT

IN NORSE MYTHOLOGY, HEIÐRÚN WAS A GOAT WHOSE UDDERS PRODUCED MEAD.

Beer. It always seems like such a good idea at the time, doesn't it? What's worse is beer seems like an even better idea after you've had some beer.

STEVEN HALL

REASON #41

YOU CAN'T WET THE BABY'S HEAD WITH ORANGE JUICE.

BEER FACT

IN THE 13TH CENTURY, POPE GREGORY IX DECREED THAT BAPTISMS BY BEER WERE INVALID.

Beer, if drunk with moderation, softens the temper, cheers the spirit and promotes health.

THOMAS JEFFERSON

I did quite enjoy the days when one went for a beer at one's local in Paris and woke up in Corsica.

PETER O'TOOLE

REASON #42

15 MINUTES LATE IS STILL EARLY IN MY BOOK.

BEER FACT

KARL MARX DECLARED BEER TO BE THE 'STAPLE FOOD OF MUNICH'.

Whiskey's too tough, Champagne costs too much,
Vodka puts my mouth in gear.
I hope this refrain, Will help me explain,
As a matter of fact, I like beer.

TOM T. HALL

REASON #43

I'M SURE THEY'RE ONLY TESTING THE FIRE ALARM.

BEER FACT

Pub-goers used to have ceramic cups with a whistle in the rim. When empty, they requested service by using the whistle, leading to the phrase 'Wet your whistle'.

BEER HE DRANK – SEVEN GOBLETS. HIS SPIRIT WAS LOOSENED. HE BECAME HILARIOUS.

FROM THE *EPIC OF GILGAMESH*, 3000 BC

REASON #44

THE FIRST FIVE DAYS AFTER THE WEEKEND ARE THE HARDEST.

BEER FACT

In 1985, former England football captain Emlyn Hughes recorded a 60-minute cassette called 'Homebrewing Made Easy'.

Beer's intellectual. What a shame so many idiots drink it.

RAY BRADBURY

A quart of ale is a dish for a king.

WILLIAM SHAKESPEARE, *A WINTER'S TALE*

REASON #45

DECORATING
IS ALL IN THE
PREPARATION.
THIS IS HOW I PREPARE.

BEER FACT

CANS HAVE NO EFFECT ON THE TASTE OF BEER – POUR IT INTO A GLASS FIRST AND YOU WON'T BE ABLE TO TELL THE DIFFERENCE.

Beauty is in the eye of the beer holder.

KINKY FRIEDMAN

I got drunk last night and my house wasn't where I left it.

REASON #46

MY TEAM WON*
MY TEAM LOST*
MY TEAM DREW*

*DELETE AS APPLICABLE

BEER FACT

GERMANS CALL DRUNK PEOPLE BIERLEICHEN, OR 'BEER CORPSES'.

St George he was for England,
And before he killed the dragon
He drank a pint of English ale
Out of an English flagon.

G. K. CHESTERTON

REASON #47
BECAUSE BEER IS THE ANSWER. EVEN THOUGH I CAN'T REMEMBER THE QUESTION.

BEER FACT

'KOLCHBIER' IS A PROTECTED NAME. IT CAN ONLY BE MADE BY A MEMBER OF THE KOLN BREWERS UNION.

*May your Guardian Angel be at your side
to pick ya up off the floor,
And hand ya another cold stout from the store.*

IRISH TOAST

REASON #48

WHO NEEDS SIX-PACK ABS? I'M GOING FOR A BARREL.

BEER FACT

The Chinese brewed a beer during the Tang dynasty (618–907) called 'p'ei', otherwise known as 'floating ants'.

Always skip to the pub to enjoy your barley and hops.

BENNY BELLAMACINA

The best beer in the world is the one you're holding in your hand.

JANELL HARRIS

REASON #49

IT WILL MAKE MY ARGUMENTS FAULTLESS.

BEER FACT

THE POLISH BEER-LOVERS' PARTY (PPPP – POLSKA PARTIA PRZYJACIÓŁ PIWA) WON 16 SEATS IN THE 1991 PARLIAMENTARY ELECTIONS.

What is civilization if it isn't people talking to each other over a goddamned beer?

JAMES S. A. COREY,
CIBOLA BURN

Drink? Die! Drink not? Die anyhow! Therefore, drink!

GERMAN PROVERB

REASON #50

IT'S BEER
- THAT'S REASON ENOUGH ITSELF.

BEER FACT

James Joule, after whom the unit of energy is named, was a brewery manager – science was his hobby.

In wine there is wisdom, in beer there is freedom, in water there is bacteria.

BENJAMIN FRANKLIN

I look like the kind of guy who has a bottle of beer in my hand.

CHARLES BRONSON

REASON #51

IT'S WHY I GOT UP THIS AFTERNOON.

BEER FACT

In his satirical pictures, William Hogarth portrayed the inhabitants of 'Beer Street' as happy and healthy and those who lived in 'Gin Lane' as slaves to an addiction.

Beer – a high and mighty liquor.

JULIUS CAESAR

I have a beer belly.

CHRISTY TURLINGTON

REASON #52

EXPERIMENTING
WITH NEW BEERS
QUALIFIES ME FOR A
NOBEL PRIZE.

BEER FACT

LOUIS PASTEUR PUBLISHED A PAMPHLET THAT OUTLINED THE CAUSES OF BEER SPOILAGE AND METHODS TO PREVENT IT.

Have you tried the beer called Trestle Table? Drink two pints and your legs fold underneath you.

What do you get when you put root beer into a square glass?
Beer

REASON #53

I DIDN'T GET
FIRED
TODAY

BEER FACT

LABOURERS THAT BUILT THE PYRAMIDS WERE PAID TEN LOAVES AND A MEASURE OF BEER A DAY.

From man's sweat and God's love, beer came into the world.

SAINT ARNOLDUS

I never drank anything stronger than beer before I was twelve.

W. C. FIELDS

REASON #54

IT'S PAYDAY.

BEER FACT

HOP FLOWERS UNDER YOUR PILLOW CAN HELP WITH A GOOD NIGHT'S SLEEP.

God made yeast, as well as dough, and loves fermentation just as dearly as he loves vegetation.

RALPH WALDO EMERSON

My idea of childcare at festivals is to sit at a trestle table with an ale while the kids run around and make up their own games.

TOM HODGKINSON

REASON #55

MY TASTE BUDS HAVE BEEN GOOD ALL WEEK AND DESERVE A TREAT.

BEER FACT

BEER TASTES MORE BITTER ON A PLANE AS OUR ABILITY TO TASTE SWEETNESS IS IMPAIRED ABOVE 35,000 FEET.

I would give all my fame for a pot of ale, and safety.

WILLIAM SHAKESPEARE,
KING HENRY V

A fine beer may be judged with only one sip, but it's better to be thoroughly sure.

BOHEMIAN PROVERB

REASON #56

THE ANSWER MAY NOT BE AT THE BOTTOM OF THE GLASS, BUT IT'S WORTH CHECKING.

BEER FACT

VIEILLE BON SECOURS, THE WORLD'S MOST EXPENSIVE BEER, COSTS £700 FOR A 12-LITRE BOTTLE.

What I like about playing America is you can be pretty sure you're not going to get hit with a full can of beer when you're singing and I really enjoy that!

JOE STRUMMER

REASON #57

I ONLY DRINK BEER ON DAYS BEGINNING WITH 'T' - TODAY AND TOMORROW.

BEER FACT

IF AN ANCIENT BABYLONIAN BREWED A BAD BEER, THEY WOULD BE DROWNED IN IT AS A PUNISHMENT.

I'm allergic to grass. Hey, it could be worse. I could be allergic to beer.

GREG NORMAN

The wise son brings joy to his father, but the wiser son brings beer.

MAD MORDIGAN

REASON #58

I CAN'T IGNORE 7,000 YEARS OF BREWING HISTORY.

BEER FACT

'BRAXATOR' IS THE LATIN TERM FOR A MASTER BREWER.

Everybody is using coffee; this must be prevented. His Majesty was brought up on beer, and so were both his ancestors and officers. Many battles have been fought and won by soldiers nourished on beer, and the King does not believe that coffee-drinking soldiers can be relied upon to endure hardships in case of another war.

KING FREDERICK II OF PRUSSIA

REASON #59

I NEED TO HELP THE BEERMAT FULFIL ITS RAISON D'ÊTRE.

BEER FACT

A BEERMAT COLLECTOR IS KNOWN AS A 'TEGESTOLOGIST'.

Men are simple things; they can survive a whole weekend with only three things: beer, boxer shorts and batteries for the remote control.

DIANA JORDAN

Beer has long been the prime lubricant in our social intercourse and the sacred throat-anointing fluid that accompanies the ritual of mateship.

RENNIE ELLIS

REASON #60

THE OFFICE
CCTV
CAMERA IS BROKEN.

BEER FACT

Australian Prime Minister Bob Hawke held the world record for drinking a yard of beer while at Oxford University.

He that buys land buys many stones,
He that buys flesh buys many bones,
He that buys eggs buys many shells,
But he that buys good ale buys nothing else.

JOHN RAY

REASON #61

IT'S BAD TO PROCRASTINATE - I'LL DRINK IT NOW.

BEER FACT

BEER BITTERNESS IS MEASURED IN IBUs - INTERNATIONAL BITTERNESS UNITS.

If you ever reach total enlightenment while drinking beer, I bet it makes beer shoot out your nose.

JACK HANDY

I'm going to buy a boat ... do a little travelling, and I'm going to be drinking lots of beer!

JOHN WELSH, LOTTERY WINNER

REASON #62

BECAUSE

I DON'T WANT TO LOOK BACK AND THINK 'I COULD HAVE DRUNK THAT'.

BEER FACT

The people of the Czech Republic drink the most beer – 148.6 litres per person per year. The UK rank 22nd with a humble 68.5 litres.

Beer that is not drunk has missed its vocation.

MEYER BRESLAU, DELEGATE TO THE PRUSSIAN FEDERAL STATE PARLIAMENT, 1880

REASON #63

I'M SURE A BEER RUN COUNTS AS EXERCISE.

BEER FACT

THE SUMERIANS BREWED A DIET BEER CALLED 'EB-LA', WHICH TRANSLATES AS 'LESSENS THE WAIST'.

It is a fair wind that blew men to the ale.

WASHINGTON IRVING

What's the difference between a pub and a gastro pub? About £1 per pint.

REASON #64

I'M ON A FAT-FREE AND DAIRY-FREE DIET.

BEER FACT

PUTTING A WEDGE OF LEMON OR LIME IN BEER KILLS THE HEAD AND MASKS THE FLAVOUR.

I'm starting a brewery called 'Responsibly' because everywhere you go you see 'Please Drink Responsibly'.

REASON #65

IT'S TIME FOR A
LIQUID LUNCH.

BEER FACT

A PINT OF BEER CONTAINS AROUND 4G OF B VITAMINS.

If a beer seller do not receive barley as the price of beer, but if they receive money, or make the beer measure smaller than the barley measure received, the judges shall throw the brewer into the water.

THE CODE OF HAMMURABI, 1500-2000 BC

REASON #66

I'M SURE IT'S AGAINST THE LAW TO WATCH THE FOOTBALL WITHOUT ONE.

BEER FACT

THERE WERE OVER 18,000 DIFFERENT CASK ALES BREWED IN THE UK IN 2014.

Fermentation may have been a greater discovery than fire.

DAVID WALLACE

There is nothing in the world like the first taste of beer.

JOHN STEINBECK

REASON #67

THE PEANUTS WOULD BE
LONELY
WITHOUT IT.

BEER FACT

THE WORLD'S OLDEST WRITTEN RECIPE IS OVER 4,000 YEARS OLD. IT'S FOR BEER.

Here's to a long life and a merry one.
A quick death and an easy one.
A pretty girl and an honest one.
A cold pint – and another one!

IRISH TOAST

REASON #68

THEY SAID 'DON'T DRINK THE WATER'.

BEER FACT

Arnold of Soissons is the patron saint of hop-pickers and Belgian brewers. In the 11th century he encouraged people to drink beer as the brewing process made it safer than water.

No poems can live long or please that are written by water-drinkers.

HORACE, 65 BC

I thought I'd have a quiet pint ... and about seventeen noisy ones.

GARETH CHILCOTT

REASON #69

THE BOTTLE OPENER IS NOT JUST ORNAMENTAL.

BEER FACT

A BEER BOTTLE COLLECTOR IS KNOWN AS A 'LABEORPHILIST'.

Froth is not beer.

DUTCH PROVERB

History flows forward on rivers of beer.

REASON #70
MY DRINKING TEAM HAS A
FOOTBALL PROBLEM.

BEER FACT

ISINGLASS IS A SUBSTANCE COMMONLY USED TO CLARIFY BEER. IT'S MADE FROM DRIED SWIM BLADDERS OF FISH.

Prohibition makes you want to cry into your beer and denies you the beer to cry into.

DON MARQUIS

He is not deserving the name of Englishman who speaketh against ale, that is, good ale.

GEORGE BORROW

REASON #71

IT'S ORGANIC,
IT MUST BE GOOD FOR ME.

BEER FACT

In the Old West, Judge Roy Bean would pass sentence (often hanging) and then serve a beer as his courthouse was also his saloon.

No, sir: there is nothing which has yet been contrived by man by which so much happiness is produced as by a good tavern or inn.

SAMUEL JOHNSON

On some days, my head is filled with such wild and original thoughts that I can barely utter a word. On other days, the brewery is closed.

FRANK VARANO

REASON #72

AS A WRITER, I NEED TO REVIEW THIS DRAUGHT.

BEER FACT

THE TERM 'ZYTHOLOGY' IS OFTEN USED FOR THE STUDY OF BEER AND BREWING.

You foam within our glasses,
you lusty golden brew,
whoever imbibes takes fire from you.
The young and the old sing your praises;
here's to beer, here's to cheer, here's to beer.

SMETANA'S 1866 OPERA *THE BARTERED BRIDE*

REASON #73

WITHOUT IT MY LIVER WOULD GET CONFUSED.

BEER FACT

In 1814, almost 400,000 gallons of beer flooded several streets in London after a huge vat ruptured in the parish of St. Giles.

There is more to life than beer alone, but beer makes those other things even better.

STEPHEN MORRIS

Beer will get you through times of no money better than money will get you through times of no beer.

FREDDIE FREAK

REASON #74

I NEED TO GET RID OF THE

TASTE

OF THE LAST ONE.

BEER FACT

BEER HOPS ARE IN THE SAME FAMILY OF FLOWERING PLANTS AS MARIJUANA.

Mother's in the kitchen washing out the jugs.
Sister's in the pantry bottling the suds.
Father's in the cellar mixin' up the hops.
Johnny's on the front porch watchin' for the cops.

PROHIBITION SONG

REASON #75
A GLASS HALF-FULL STILL NEEDS
EMPTYING.

BEER FACT

BE CAREFUL ORDERING A 'PINT'
IN SOUTH AUSTRALIA – IT'S ONLY
THREE-QUARTERS THE SIZE OF A PINT
IN THE REST OF THE COUNTRY.

*A man saw a sign outside a pub that
read 'All the beer you can drink for £5'.
He dashed in and said to the barman,
'What a great offer – give me £10 worth.'*

REASON #76

I PUT IN A 'STOUT' PERFORMANCE.

BEER FACT

STOUT IS NOT BLACK, IT'S A VERY DARK RED.

Beer may not solve your problems, but neither will water or milk.

WILEY

I'll have another beer. I'm not driving.

FATHER THEODORE, TRAPPIST MONK

REASON #77

OTHERWISE THE WORLD WILL FORGET WHAT A FIRKIN IS.

BEER FACT

The oldest commercial brewery still operating is the Weihenstephan Abbey Brewery, which has been making beer since 1040.

DOCTOR: I can't find a cause for your condition.
I think it's due to drinking.

PATIENT: Fine. I'll come back when you're sober.

REASON #78

I'M HAVING BEER AND CRISPS AT THE SAME TIME TO PROVE I CAN MULTI-TASK.

BEER FACT

STEAM BEERS ARE FERMENTED WARM LIKE ALES, BUT USE BOTTOM-FERMENTING LAGER YEAST.

My father drank beer in the morning;
later in the day he drank anything.

DEBORAH KERR AS TERRY MCKAY IN
AN AFFAIR TO REMEMBER

REASON #79

I NEED TO TEST DRIVE MY NEW PEWTER JUG.

BEER FACT

Professional beer-tasters often use white wine glasses: holding the stem prevents hand-warming the beer and the tapered shape contains the aroma.

A man who lies about beer makes enemies.

STEPHEN KING

When the arm bends, the mouth opens.

DANISH PROVERB

REASON #80

OTHERWISE THE BARMAID WOULD BE OUT OF A JOB.

BEER FACT

THE FINNISH EPIC POEM 'THE KALEVALA' CONTAINS 200 LINES ABOUT CREATION AND 400 LINES ABOUT BEER.

Most people hate the taste of beer – to begin with. It is, however, a prejudice.

WINSTON CHURCHILL

The closest thing I have to a nutritionist is the Carlsberg Beer Company.

COLIN FARRELL

REASON #81

MY WATCH SAYS IT'S BEER O'CLOCK.

BEER FACT

FOR BREAKFAST, ELIZABETH I OFTEN HAD BREAD, ALE OR WINE AND A POTTAGE MADE WITH MUTTON OR BEEF.

We could be happy if the air was as pure as beer.

RICHARD VON WEIZSAECKER, FORMER PRESIDENT OF THE GERMAN FEDERAL REPUBLIC

REASON #82

THE FORECAST SAID CLOUDY WITH A CHANCE OF BEER.

BEER FACT

THE MAYFLOWER STOPPED AT PLYMOUTH ROCK AS THE PILGRIMS HAD RUN OUT OF BEER.

Beer is the Danish national drink, and the Danish national weakness is another beer.

CLEMENTINE PADDLEFORD

The house was as empty as a beer closet in premises where painters have been at work.

MARK TWAIN

REASON #83

I'M SURE I'LL MAKE THE LAST TRAIN.

BEER FACT

THE WINNER OF THE WIFE CARRYING WORLD CHAMPIONSHIPS HELD ANNUALLY IN FINLAND RECEIVES HIS WIFE'S WEIGHT IN BEER.

For every wound, a balm.
For every sorrow, cheer.
For every storm, a calm.
For every thirst, a beer.

IRISH TOAST

REASON #84

I'M PRACTISING FOR A JOB IN QUALITY CONTROL.

BEER FACT

Shakespeare's father was an 'ale-conner', an official dedicated to ensuring the wholesomeness of bread, ale and beer.

Beer. Now there's a temporary solution.

HOMER SIMPSON

Blessed is the mother who gives birth to a brewer.

CZECH PROVERB

REASON #85

THE MILK'S GONE OFF

BEER FACT

REAL ALE NEEDS TO BE CELLARED AT BETWEEN 12 AND 14 DEGREES CENTIGRADE.

I've always thought why no one has made a women's perfume to smell like beer. I know that would turn me on.

NATE SAMPSON

Do not cease to drink beer, to eat, to intoxicate thyself, to make love, and celebrate the good days.

ANCIENT EGYPTIAN PROVERB

REASON #86

EDUCATION

IS IMPORTANT BUT BEER IS

IMPORTANTER.

BEER FACT

JOHN LUBBOCK, AN 18TH-CENTURY ENGLISH BIOLOGIST, STUDIED THE EFFECTS OF BEER ON ANTS.

How did you get those scars on your nose?

From glasses.

Have you tried contact lenses?

No - they don't hold enough beer.

REASON #87

I'M AT A BEER FESTIVAL. ON MY OWN. IN MY LIVING ROOM.

BEER FACT

MADE FROM THE MIDDLE AGES TO THE 19TH CENTURY, DEVON WHITE ALE CONTAINED RUM, FLOUR, SALT AND EGGS.

Put it back in the horse!

H. ALLEN SMITH, AN AMERICAN HUMOURIST, AFTER HE DRANK HIS FIRST AMERICAN BEER AT A BAR

REASON #88

MONEY DOESN'T BUY HAPPINESS. UNLESS YOU SPEND IT ON BEER.

BEER FACT

MORE THAN 6 MILLION PEOPLE ATTEND MUNICH'S OKTOBERFEST EVERY YEAR.

Beer is not a good cocktail-party drink, especially in a home where you don't know where the bathroom is.

BILLY CARTER, PRESIDENT JIMMY'S BROTHER

REASON #89

IT'S NOT BINGE DRINKING, IT'S A TUESDAY NIGHT.

BEER FACT

WRESTLER AND ACTOR ANDRE THE GIANT ONCE DRANK 117 BEERS IN A SINGLE SESSION.

The last swallow of lager is the worst and the last swallow of an ale is the best.

ANON

Attention: We cannot be held responsible for anything said after the third pint.

PUB SIGN

REASON #90

I'M AIMING FOR AN OBE FOR 'SERVICES TO THE BREWING INDUSTRY'.

BEER FACT

In the 1960s Revlon marketed a cologne called 'Pub' with the slogan 'Give it to him. And let a little rub off on you.'

Nothing ever tasted better than a cold beer on a beautiful afternoon with nothing to look forward to than more of the same.

HUGH HOOD

Thought of giving it all away, to a registered charity. All I need is a pint a day.

**PAUL MCCARTNEY,
BAND ON THE RUN**

REASON #91

MY SAT NAV IS STUCK ON 'PUB'.

BEER FACT

Years ago when pub-goers became rowdy, the landlord would shout 'Settle down – mind your pints and quarts' which over time became 'Mind your Ps and Qs'.

Religions change; beer and wine remain.

HERVEY ALLEN

Beer is an improvement on water itself.

GRANT JOHNSON

REASON #92

THE PINT GLASS BALANCES THE DARTS IN THE OTHER HAND.

BEER FACT

BEER CONTAINS AT LEAST 40 DIFFERENT PROTEINS, MAKING UP TO 2G OF EACH PINT.

I think this would be a good time for a beer.

FRANKLIN D. ROOSEVELT, UPON SIGNING A BILL THAT PAVED THE WAY TO REPEAL PROHIBITION

REASON #93

BEER IS MADE FROM GRAINS AND HOPS, SO REALLY IT'S A LIQUID SALAD.

BEER FACT

IN THE 15TH CENTURY, ENGLISH BREWERS CALLED HOPS 'WHICKED WEED'.

The church is near, but the road is icy. The bar is far away, but I will walk carefully.

RUSSIAN PROVERB

It's not about drinking a dozen beers – it's about enjoying the one you have in your hand.

ANON

REASON #94

I'M DOING MY BIT TO CONSERVE WATER.

BEER FACT

India Pale Ales were traditionally highly alcoholic to preserve the beer during its long voyage from England to the troops in India.

I've only been in love with a beer bottle and a mirror.

SID VICIOUS

Who cares how time advances? I am drinking ale today.

EDGAR ALLAN POE

REASON #95

OTHERWISE THE BARLEY DIED FOR NOTHING.

BEER FACT

IF YOU HAVE A GLUTEN ALLERGY, YOU MAY END UP WITH A BEER MADE WITH QUINOA.

Light beer is an invention of the Prince of Darkness.

COLIN DEXTER, INSPECTOR MORSE

When the hour is nigh me, Let me in a tavern die, With a tankard by me.

CONFESIO, 12TH-CENTURY POET

REASON #96

MY FAVOURITE SONG IS 'ALEHOUSE ROCK'.

BEER FACT

VIKINGS WOULD DOWN SUBSTANTIAL QUANTITIES OF A HEATHER BEER THEY CALLED 'AUL' BEFORE CHARGING INTO BATTLE.

Give a man a beer, waste an hour. Teach a man to brew, and waste a lifetime.

BILL OWEN

No soldier can properly fight unless he is properly fed on beef and beer.

JOHN CHURCHILL, 1ST DUKE OF MARLBOROUGH

REASON #97

THE KIDS ARE
FINALLY
IN BED.

BEER FACT

'SMALL BEER' WAS A LOW-ALCOHOL BREW IN MEDIEVAL TIMES, RESERVED FOR SERVANTS AND CHILDREN.

Whiskey and beer are a man's worst enemies ... but the man that runs away from his enemies is a coward!

ZECA PAGODINHO, BRAZILIAN SONGWRITER

REASON #98

IN DOG BEERS,

I'VE ONLY HAD ONE SO FAR THIS EVENING.

BEER FACT

The process for making sake, the Japanese rice wine, is more like brewing beer than traditional wine making.

IT COMES IN PINTS?

PETER JACKSON

REASON #99

I'M PREVENTING THIRST, AND PREVENTION IS BETTER THAN CURE.

BEER FACT

DUBLIN WATER HAS INCREASED CALCIUM CHLORIDE LEVELS WHICH ENHANCE THE FLAVOURS OF DARK STOUTS.

Life alas, is very drear.
Up with the glass, down
with the beer!

LOUIS UNTERMEYER

[I recommend] bread,
meat, vegetables
and beer.

SOPHOCLES

REASON #100

I'M IN WITH THE

INN

CROWD

BEER FACT

*The Incas fermented beer by ch...
corn and spitting it out. The enzym...
saliva started the fermentation p...*

*Payday came and
with it beer.*

RUDYARD KIPLING

*My favourite
tan is a 'mothe
mixture of stou*

REASON #101

I EXPECTED THAT ITEM IN THE BAGGING AREA.

BEER FACT

THE LATIN NAME OF THE COMMON HOP IS 'HUMULUS LUPULUS' WHICH TRANSLATES AS 'SMALL HUMBLE WOLF'.

A mouth of a perfectly happy man is filled with beer.

ANCIENT EGYPTIAN PROVERB

APPENDIX 1

THE HISTORY OF BEER

A Timeline

7000 BC – *The earliest known beer production begins*

Before I was born – *Something about Bavarian Purity Laws*

Now

Bloody ages – *Next pint*

APPENDIX 2
HANGOVERS AROUND THE WORLD

Before the word 'hangover' came along, we used to describe
the feeling we had the morning after the night before as 'crapulous'.
Here's how some beer drinkers around the world describe it now.

El Salvador	Estoy de goma	Made of rubber
France	Avoir la gueule de bois	Have a wooden mouth
Germany	Einer kater haben	Have a tom-cat
Hungary	Másnaposság	Next-day-ish-ness
Japan	Futsukayoi	Two day drunk
Mexico	Cruda	Raw
Norway	Jeg har tommermen	I have carpenters
Spain	Resaca	Backwash
Sweden	Baksmalla	Smacked from behind
Vietnam	D·ung xiên	Built cockeyed

APPENDIX 3

THE WATER CYCLE

 1. Evaporation

 2. Condensation

 3. Precipitation

 4. Accumulation

 5. Fermentation

 6. Celebration

 7. Micturation

If you've got the stamina for another round, why not try...

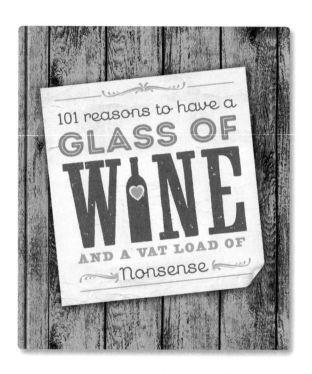